STRIDE FOR STRIDE

THE LIONS IN NEW ZEALAND 2017

Mick Cleary
& Ian Robertson

Pictures by
Getty Images

Quotes edited and introduced by
Chris Jones

———————————————

Published in the UK in 2017 by
Lennard Publishing, an imprint of
Lennard Associates Ltd,
Mackerye End,
Harpenden, Herts AL5 5DR
email: orders@lennardqap.co.uk

Distributed by G2 Entertainment
c/o Orca Book Services
160 Eastern Avenue, Milton Park
Abingdon, OX14 4SB

ISBN: 978-1-78281-811-3

Production editor: Chris Marshall
Text and cover design: Paul Cooper

Printed and bound in Italy
by L.E.G.O. S.p.A

INITIAL EXCHANGES

'There is no point any of us getting on the plane if we don't think we can beat the All Blacks' was the Gatland refrain that was to be heard many times prior to departure

The Lions players looked in the zone. In fact, a few of them were asleep, nodding off en route to the opening game against the Provincial Barbarians in Whangarei, a measure of the arduous nature of the entire trip. That first match was only three days after the 41-man touring party had landed in Auckland, 72 hours of unpacking and settling and training. And sleeping if you were lucky.

That snapshot of players battling to overcome significant odds was an image that encapsulated the tour. 'Mission Impossible' as it was deemed by many. A 'suicidal' itinerary in the words of former All Blacks and Lions head coach Sir Graham Henry. Yet there was none of that air of tilting against windmills when Warren Gatland unveiled his touring squad in mid-April. Gatland had been here before. He was a Kiwi, too, one who had played (and scored) against the Lions for his native Waikato in 1993. Gatland knew how much the trip meant to New Zealanders. And if it meant that much to them, as it did for the simple reason that it was a once-in-a-career experience, a 12-year build-up to a six-week shoot-out, then it had to mean as much to every single one of the Lions players. Not just for the memory of touring but for believing that they could win. 'There is no point any of us getting on the plane if we don't think we can beat the All Blacks' was the Gatland refrain that was to be heard many times prior to departure.

Gatland, on his third Lions tour, his second as head coach, having led the team to success in Australia four years earlier, knew exactly what it would take. Time has always been the enemy of the Lions. There

simply isn't enough of it. And in this ever-congested and conflicted world, there was even less of it available for this trip. That is why Gatland was faithful to those he knew best: on his coaching panel in the form of Andy Farrell and Graham Rowntree, alongside head of strength and conditioning Paul 'Bobby' Stridgeon; in his captain, Sam Warburton; and in those players who had either toured with the Lions before or whom Gatland had observed at close quarters across the preceding 12 months.

The Aviva Premiership and PRO12 finals were on Saturday 27 May; a farewell dinner the following day before the long trek south (via a stopover in Melbourne) for arrival in New Zealand on Wednesday. No wonder the Lions found it hard to put away their first opponents, a scratch side like themselves, drawn from all the 15 provincial unions and considered by far the weakest opposition the Lions would face on their ten-match trip. Gatland was very familiar with one of the Barbarians, fly half son Bryn, who was lively and inventive, almost guiding his side to a famous victory, only for the Lions to rouse themselves, relatively so, after the interval to come through 13-7 courtesy of a second-half try from Anthony Watson, having trailed 7-3 at the break.

Gatland had pledged that everyone would get a start across the first three games and he was true to his word even though it was clear that the Lions were struggling to find their feet. They were pilloried by the New Zealand media after their stuttering opening, legitimate criticism which turned into something altogether nastier and more self-indulgent later in the tour. There was to be no let-up in the schedule, with the ad hoc Barbarians, several of whom were

> **BELOW** Sonny Bill Williams reaches out to touch down for the Blues as the Lions come unstuck at Eden Park in match two.
>
> **FACING PAGE** Stuart Hogg after suffering a tour-ending facial fracture in a collision with Conor Murray's elbow against the Crusaders.
>
> **PAGE 3** Wing Anthony Watson scores a second-half try as the Lions win the tour curtain-raiser against the Provincial Barbarians.

part-timers, followed by a wham-bam line-up of Super Rugby franchises, starting with the Blues in Auckland, with the Crusaders, Highlanders and the Chiefs flexing muscles behind them. The only break in that Super sequence came on the Saturday prior to the first Test when the Maori All Blacks lay in wait in Rotorua, in essence a fourth Test for the Lions.

There was to be no griping, no moaning, just a determination to get on with it. And the Lions did, pledging faith in the project despite the early signs of stress and difficulty. Behind the scenes the Lions insisted that training was going well, that combinations were being developed and the game plan honed. On the evidence of the second game, a loss to the Blues at Eden Park, it appeared to be putting a gloss on a worrying reality. The Blues were far from the strongest of the franchises, but with the likes of new wing sensation Rieko Ioane and global superstar Sonny Bill Williams in their ranks they had plenty of firepower. Ioane was to be promoted through the ranks to win his first start on the strength of what he delivered for the Blues. A sharp-eyed, fleet-footed case study in finishing, his pace was enough to do for the Lions defence, which was caught napping and on its heels as the 20-year-old scored within seven minutes of the start, Sonny Bill adding another on the stroke of half-time. The Lions did get across the try line through CJ Stander, and the boot of Leigh Halfpenny did keep them in the contest with three penalties and a conversion, but the Blues continued to press and came through 22-16, Ihaia West scoring the decisive try in the 73rd minute.

The Lions knew that by the time they returned to Eden Park for the first Test in just over a fortnight's time they would have to be an altogether tougher, more composed and cohesive unit. It was a formidable task ahead of them as they packed bags for the island-hopping flight to Christchurch.

A Lions tour often throws up extremes of emotion as well as of criticism. It is an intense experience and the character of the players, their ability to withstand external pressure as well as quell any inner doubts, is the key consideration. Gatland was aware of that, but if he needed any succour himself it was to come pretty quickly in the guise of a tour-shaping victory over the mighty Crusaders. The scoreline may only have been 12-3 (testimony to the aggressive line speed of the Lions defence, which was to become such a feature of the tour, as well as to the tricky weather conditions) but it was a notable triumph against a team that had swept all before them up to that point. It was a reflection of the quality of the Lions defence that this was the first time in 37 games that the Crusaders had been kept to three points. On such performances are judgments made, and the Lions

> **BELOW** Skipper Sam Warburton scores his side's third try against the Highlanders, but the Lions were unable to hold on to a 22-13 lead.
>
> **RIGHT** Referee Jaco Peyper signals a Lions try, scored by Maro Itoje, as the tourists beat the Maori All Blacks 32-10 in Rotorua.

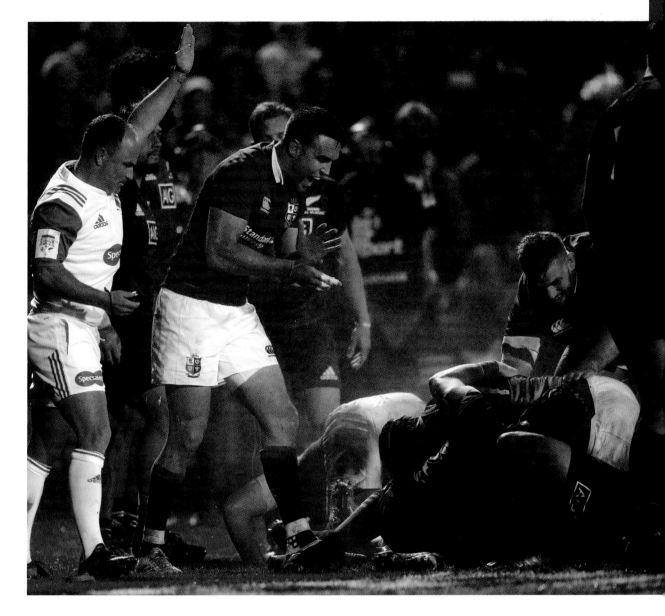

management headed on to Dunedin for their next assignment buoyed by the thought that their defensive patterns were taking shape. There was also a heartening upturn in form for Johnny Sexton, the Irish fly half who had had an underwhelming start to the tour but who made the most of his time when coming on as an early replacement and lining up alongside (the starting) Owen Farrell.

The switchback nature of the pre-Test games continued, from the Christchurch spike to a deflating late loss, 23-22, at the enclosed Forsyth Barr Stadium in Dunedin. If the swelling clans of Lions fans found solace in the roof-encased stadium, protection against the chill, sleeting rain, there was understandable concern that a 22-13 lead in the 53rd minute was wasted as the Highlanders came back with a try from Liam Coltman converted by Marty Banks, who then landed a penalty to secure victory.

There is no benefit in dwelling on losses with the next game only three days away in Rotorua. The Maori All Blacks are a cherished side in New Zealand, rooted deep in the history of the country and with a record that matches their status. If the Lions were in need of a boost seven days from the first Test, they were to receive it with an empathic performance that resulted in 32-10 victory. It was a result that announced the 2017 Lions as a side of great heart and togetherness, fit and proper opposition for the Test series against the back-to-back world champions.

INITIAL EXCHANGES: POINTS OF VIEW

The slow start to the tour was quickened by the hugely significant win over the Crusaders, and even though the midweek team was again beaten in Dunedin, the Saturday side travelled to Rotorua to face the Maori All Blacks with confidence. Johnny Sexton was preferred to Owen Farrell at fly half.

'Johnny needs some more rugby and he's got a bit of his mojo back, so we wanted to give him a start,' said Warren Gatland, only for Farrell to withdraw from the bench a matter of hours later with a quad injury.

Another selection conundrum involved the captain. Sam Warburton always faced a race against time to be fit for the first Test with a knee injury, followed by an ankle niggle, and was again left out of the starting XV for the Maori clash.

'This tour isn't about Sam Warburton, it's about putting the squad first, so if he isn't involved in the first Test he will fully understand that,' Gatland explained.

As for the Maori, they may have been a scratch side, but were still bursting with All Blacks talent such as Rieko Ioane and Nehe Milner-Skudder.

'We recognise the challenge that is ahead of us on Saturday, but we're really excited as a group by the opportunity we have to represent New Zealand, Maoridom and the fans that will descend on Rotorua this weekend,' said Maori head coach Colin Cooper.

Despite the passion of the Rotorua crowd and the talent in the Maori ranks, the Lions were far too strong, crushing Cooper's side by 32 points to 10 in filthy conditions, as the Test side started to take shape.

After the game Gatland cranked up the heat on opposite number Steve Hansen, who had been vocal in the media up to this point.

'He's been doing a lot of press conferences and I can only take that as a sign of respect in that he is a little bit worried,' Gatland said. 'We've been written off, and it's brought us closer together as a group.'

Gatland was also forced to defend his selection of the Geography Six, a group of players called up to the squad over the weekend because of logistical convenience.

'My job is to win a Test series and I will do whatever it takes to do that,' the Kiwi added defiantly.

BELOW Lions head coach Warren Gatland and his tour captain Sam Warburton at a press conference in Dunedin.

FIRST TEST

Jonathan Davies was in support, fed Daly who leaned in and then out, the ball coming back infield – and just as Davies was gang-tackled, there was Sean O'Brien in support to score

The British & Irish Lions returned to Eden Park after their losing skirmish against the Blues a fortnight earlier fortified by their own defiant performances on the field of play as well as by the swelling numbers of the Red Army. The projected thousands had indeed materialised in a bid to threaten the status of Eden Park as a fortress. The All Blacks had not lost there since 1994, but they had never played there in front of so many opposition supporters, rendering the venue a neutral backdrop in terms of noise and colour.

Yet all concerned knew that it would take far more than mere vocals if the world champions were to be defeated. New Zealand had registered 37 straight wins in Auckland and had lost only once, to Ireland in Chicago, since retaining the Rugby World Cup at Twickenham in 2015. They were a formidable opponent, as they had shown to alarming effect when running 12 tries past a stunned Samoa in a warm-up Test at the self-same venue eight days earlier. If that were not worrying enough for Lions fans, that team was boosted by the return from injury (broken thumb) of No. 8 and captain Kieran Read. The All Blacks were effectively at full strength, with only hooker Dane Coles, a long-term absentee (concussion), missing from the ranks.

The Lions, though, were not in bad order themselves. They had lost Stuart Hogg to a freak accident earlier in the tour but had come through fairly unscathed. They had also had a spring in their step after impressive back-to-back victories over the Maori All Blacks and then the Chiefs in Hamilton. That final game

in Warren Gatland's home town helped shape selection, with two notable performances from Liam Williams and Elliot Daly seeing them go straight into the starting XV. The 34-6 win had featured a try-of-the-tour effort from Jack Nowell, a movement started by a darting run from Daly. Nowell touched down twice on the night with Jared Payne also on the scoresheet. A penalty try was also awarded after a drive towards the line was pulled down. The match was also newsworthy for Gatland's decision to summon half a dozen players – to be dubbed the 'Geography Six' – to sit on the bench for the Chiefs match (and again for the midweek game against the Hurricanes in Wellington) in order to spare the Test squad from having to double up as replacements during the lead-in. The players were chosen not on merit but by location, four of them, Gareth Davies, Cory Hill,

Kristian Dacey and Tomas Francis, already being in Auckland on the Wales tour, while the two Scottish call-ups, Finn Russell and Allan Dell, only had to make a quick flit over from Australia. It was a contentious decision by Gatland, potentially destabilising, but the head coach remained steadfast in the face of criticism. There had been murmurings even within the camp and, if anything, with Gatland later acknowledging that it may not have been the right call, the situation perhaps served to draw everyone that bit closer.

The fact that tour captain Sam Warburton did not make the Test starting line-up had been signalled well in advance, the Wales flanker battling to get back up to match sharpness after a lengthy lay-off prior to departure. Instead it was Munster back-row forward Peter O'Mahony who had the honour of leading the Lions down the Eden Park tunnel, a swift about-turn in fortunes for the well-regarded Munsterman, who had been on bench duty for the final game of the 2017 Six Nations Championship, only to be summoned in the warm-up and go on to produce a man-of-the-match performance as England's Grand Slam was prevented.

O'Mahony needed all his leadership skills to keep his men upbeat after sustaining tremendous pressure throughout the first half. It was a trademark All Black performance, with energy and pace at its heart. The Lions had their chances but were profligate. New Zealand were not. There was an indication of the pattern of the match from the early stages. A portent of the Lions' wastefulness came within two minutes of the start. Jonathan Davies made a big bust up through the middle and had scrum half Conor Murray in support who looked strong but was brought down by a last-gasp tap-tackle from Aaron Smith. Even so, the Lions managed to sustain the attack, moving left from where Elliot Daly tried to spiral in at the corner but was denied by Israel Dagg. On such margins might Test matches be decided.

In the 17th minute New Zealand showed how it should be done. They were awarded a penalty within easy range of the posts. Within the blink of any eye, Aaron Smith had tapped the ball, spun it right, through the hands of Beauden Barrett and Israel Dagg and on to hooker Codie Taylor, who had a relatively easy run-in. Simple and quick – three passes to touchdown. Taylor was supposed to be a (relative) frailty in that he was not injured hooker Dane Coles. Yet he took the ball cleanly, picking it off his toes with the assurance of a back-line player, and scored in the corner with Daly caught napping.

That was to be the tale of the evening – the All Blacks sharp-minded and potent; the Lions playing off the back foot, struggling to really make a mark. Well, that is, apart from one moment of magic that spawned the try of the series, a score to rank with the 'try from the end of the world' scored by France's Jean-Luc Sadourny on the occasion of New Zealand's last defeat at Eden Park in 1994. Sean O'Brien's finishing effort will likely not gain such status in folklore as it was scored in a losing cause, but it bore all the hallmarks of that famous try 23 years earlier.

It was always felt that the selection of Liam Williams at full back over the more dependable Leigh Halfpenny was something of a gamble, trading possible defensive frailty for counterattacking potential. And so it proved on the night, Williams' mesmerising run setting in motion an electrifying sequence five minutes before the half-time break. Anthony Watson fielded a kick in his own 22 and threw it infield, putting his team-mate under pressure. Williams set off, past one, past two and on and on he surged. Jonathan Davies was in support, fed Daly who leaned in and then out, the ball coming back infield – and just as Davies was gang-tackled, there was Sean O'Brien in support to score.

It was only the All Blacks that were supposed to be capable of such rugby, of such verve and imagination and daring. It was a try for the memory vault. Williams did show the other side of his game when missing a high ball, an error that led to Rieko Ioane's second try in the 69th minute, the young wing getting a somewhat fortunate bounce and away he went. Ioane had touched down for his first try in the 54th minute, Read showing just why he has been considered the pre-eminent No. 8 in world rugby over the past few years when somehow flicking the ball clear from a disintegrating scrum to enable Aaron Smith to move the ball to the left flank from where Ioane went in at the corner. The Lions did not fold, Rhys Webb getting a late touchdown to put a certain respectability on the scoreboard, but they were well beaten.

There were stand-out New Zealand performances from lock Brodie Retallick, a ceaseless presence, and open-side Sam Cane, putting in a shift reminiscent of Richie McCaw himself. New Zealand even managed to endure the loss of two back-line players in the first half – Ben Smith to a head injury, and centre Ryan Crotty limping off.

The Lions had been valiant, with a strong performance from Jonathan Davies in the centre and Ben Te'o showing well alongside. The decision to opt for the experience of Alun Wyn Jones over the precocious talent of Maro Itoje, who impressed from the bench, looked flawed. The Lions did as expected in many regards, being dogged and resourceful, but they could not match the excellence of the All Blacks in converting opportunities. The Eden Park citadel stood firm.

FIRST TEST: POINTS OF VIEW

From Rotorua the Lions headed to Hamilton with a spring in their step for the midweek meeting with the Chiefs, a matter of days before the first Test against the All Blacks. All six of the controversial late call-ups – Allan Dell, Kristian Dacey, Tomas Francis, Cory Hill, Gareth Davies and Finn Russell – were named on the bench.

'We are here to win a Test series and we have brought cover for the replacements' bench so we can limit the number of players who need to double up, which is tough to do at this level of rugby,' Gatland said.

'Those involved on Tuesday will be playing not only for themselves in terms of further selection but also for the whole squad.'

Ireland hooker Rory Best was named as captain, shortly after being awarded an OBE in the Queen's Birthday Honours List.

'There has been fun but there has been a lot of sincere congratulations too. The lads have all congratulated me and it means a lot,' said Best.

Best's men overwhelmed the highly fancied Chiefs by 34 points to 6, with the likes of Elliot Daly, Jack Nowell and Liam Williams playing their way into Test contention.

'I hope we are peaking at the right time. We always felt that we would get better the longer we spent together,' Gatland said.

A few days later, Gatland sprang a selection surprise, starting Williams and Daly in the back three for the series opener in Auckland.

As expected, tour skipper Warburton was on the bench, with Munster and Ireland flanker Peter O'Mahony named as captain.

'We have picked a side based on form with a lot of players putting their hands up,' said Gatland.

BELOW Liam Williams in full lfight as he instigates Sean O'Brien's try for the Lions in the first Test at Eden Park.

SECOND TEST

The Lions may have had a plan for keeping Sonny Bill Williams quiet, but they had no need of it as the New Zealand centre put himself out of the game with a shoulder charge into the head of Anthony Watson

W hen the Lions arrived in New Zealand they already knew that they would have to scale mountain peaks as formidable as those that grace the Queenstown landscape they were due to visit after they had finished their sporting business in Wellington. That range is called The Remarkables and such an epitaph would be sure to be inscribed on any future monument to their 2017 tour were they to pull off an against-the-odds victory at the Westpac Stadium where New Zealand had not been beaten since England triumphed there in 2003 a few months before they were to win the Rugby World Cup. Only two teams in the

ABOVE Iain Henderson (left) is yellow-carded against the Hurricanes, an untimely indiscretion, perhaps, since he was in contention for a Test place.

FACING PAGE Although he converted seven kicks in the second Test, Beauden Barrett missed a further three kickable chances.

PAGE 15 Turning point. Sonny Bill Williams charges into Anthony Watson, an infringement that earned the All Black centre a red card.

history of the Lions had come back from a 1-0 deficit to claim a series victory: the touring party of 1899 and one of more recent vintage, Finlay Calder's side of 1989 in Australia.

The stats were against the Lions, that is for sure. And they still had another match to navigate, against defending Super Rugby champions the Hurricanes. If that was a daunting prospect, at least it would be offset by the fact that for the only time on the tour the Lions were based in the same place for seven days – a time to recuperate and to recharge. It is at such moments that Lions tours can either sink or soar. The weeks of endless guff about bonding and the power of the jersey, the power of the collective over and above the spur of individual ambition, all boiled down to weeks like these. This is when tours are defined for ill or for better, when players reveal themselves to be individuals of substance or not.

In that regard the midweek battlers did the Lions proud, doing all that was within their remit to deliver against the Hurricanes, only to fall foul of the 65th-minute sin-binning of lock Iain Henderson for a dangerous clear-out of Jordie Barrett, a significant blemish in terms of the run of the game as well as a blot on the Ulsterman's copybook, which had made for splendid reading up to that point. Henderson's enforced absence was compounded by the ongoing situation of the Geography Six, that band of back-ups whom Gatland had decreed (under pressure from his own squad) should only be used as actual replacements in extreme circumstances, primarily injury. Meanwhile, those in the squad who did service at the coal face, such as the entire front row of Joe Marler, Rory Best and Dan Cole, knew that their shift for the midweek side would effectively rule them out of contention for the Test team.

Yet again, though, there were to be call-ups from the midweekers to cover bench duties four days later. Courtney Lawes had been in fine fettle throughout the tour, only for his cause to be stymied by a head injury, but the Northampton man showed that he was in prime form, featuring strongly against the Hurricanes before being replaced in the 53rd minute by George Kruis, who was to be dropped from the Test side for his Saracens team-mate Maro Itoje.

The Lions would probably have secured another victory if they had used their bench as they might normally have done. Once again they showed impressive fortitude and touches as they breezed to a 23-7 lead at half-time thanks to tries from wings Tommy Seymour and George North, the boot of Dan Biggar supplying the other points. The Lions were leading 31-17 when Henderson had his moment of recklessness, allowing the Hurricanes to come right back into it with converted tries from Wes Goosen and Vaea Fifita – and almost snatch victory with a near-miss effort.

Gatland knew what he wanted from his men. The head coach had given his forward pack a public hurry-up in the aftermath of the first Test, bemoaning the fact that the Lions had been outmuscled by their opponents. 'We need to toughen ourselves, to be more physical' was the blunt assessment. The Lions had allowed the All Blacks to dominate the breakdown and dictate the shape and rhythm of the match by playing close off scrum half Aaron Smith.

To that end, Gatland made two significant changes in the pack, restoring Sam Warburton to the starting XV, but on the blind side in place of O'Mahony so that Sean O'Brien could continue to do his stuff on the open side. There was a change at lock, too, the only surprise being that it was Alun Wyn Jones who was retained, Kruis making way for the elevation of Itoje.

The real surprise came in the midfield axis, with Johnny Sexton being paired with Owen Farrell at the expense of Ben Te'o, who dropped to the bench. The combination had played in tandem already, Sexton coming on early against the Crusaders because of an injury as the Lions impressed in victory over New Zealand's leading franchise and featuring also in the closing stages of the first Test in Auckland. The dual

playmaker strategy has proven worth, as England have shown with the axis of George Ford and Farrell, the idea being to use their vision and distribution to play the field through their tactical kicking as well as in feeding the outside backs. Liam Williams' vivid counterattack at Eden Park that instigated the length-of-the-field try finished by Sean O'Brien was a moment of inspiration (or of desperation) and Gatland clearly wanted to bring his strike runners into the game more often.

It was a bold move. But it all came to fruition even if it was to be circumstance that had the telling impact on the game. The Lions may have had a plan for keeping Sonny Bill Williams quiet, but they had no need of it as the New Zealand centre put himself out of the game in the 24th minute with a shoulder charge into the head of Anthony Watson as he brought the ball back. It was a brave call by referee Jérôme Garcès, and the right one. It was high and reckless, a perfect example of good use of technology to discern just how bad it was.

It was the first dismissal of an All Black in a Test match in 50 years. Yet the Lions struggled to make best use of their numerical advantage. It took them until the closing quarter to make that putative superiority tell, with tries from Toby Faletau and Conor Murray helping to see them through to an historic 24-21 victory. Even then it took a nerve-shredding penalty kick from Owen Farrell in the 77th minute to seal the deal, a rather harsh call against prop Charlie Faumuina for a tackle on Kyle Sinckler giving the Lions their opportunity. Farrell did not miss a beat as he nailed the kick, in stark contrast to Beauden Barrett who had a wobbly night in missing three straightforward pots at goal. The fly half did land seven kicks, but it was not enough as the Lions finally gathered themselves in the closing stages after a dreadful third quarter in which they conceded seven penalties and looked as if they were going to blow a golden chance.

It was the forward pack, though, that rose to the challenge. They had been emasculated in Auckland, their machismo questioned. They responded. It was a huge night for Alun Wyn Jones, so often a warrior for

Wales but a jaded force at Eden Park. Others had legitimate claim on the shirt. But it belonged to Jones, playing in his eighth straight Lions Test. And he delivered, giving off the right vibes from the first whistle. The pack had to make the All Blacks work. And they did. Tadhg Furlong rumbled, so too did Sean O'Brien. There was a wholly different feel about the Lions. They were up for the fight, proactive rather than reactive and passive. Maro Itoje showed just why he ought to have started in Auckland – busy and bothersome.

Much rested on Sam Warburton. Never mind his role as Lions captain – solid and steadfast. What the Lions needed was not persona nor words but deeds at the breakdown. And they got them. The back row was notably influential.

Faletau came through strongly to help the Lions overcome the loss of Mako Vunipola to the sin-bin in the 55th minute for an illegal clear-out on Beauden Barrett at a ruck. On the hour the Lions went right, where Anthony Watson made good ground, back left where Liam Williams fed Toby Faletau who had much to do. And he did it, crashing through Israel Dagg to score a try of which any marksman would have been proud. It was a terrific finish.

Barrett did stretch New Zealand's lead again with a penalty in the 66th minute, only for the Lions to come again, an angled run by hooker Jamie George creating enough havoc in All Blacks ranks for Murray to spot the opening and take it. Farrell converted then landed his penalty, and a landmark victory was in the record books.

SECOND TEST: POINTS OF VIEW

The simmering animosity between the two coaches started to boil over in the aftermath of the first Test, with Lions boss Warren Gatland accusing the All Blacks of deliberately trying to injure his scrum half Conor Murray. Steve Hansen was far from impressed, labelling his counterpart 'predictable and desperate'. 'What he's implying is we are deliberately going out to injure somebody, and that's not the case. I guess he might be a bit desperate,' Hansen said. 'It's another predictable comment coming from Gats. He is looking to take the heat off his own team.'

Before the second Test, the Lions were first at the Westpac Stadium to face the Hurricanes, with Gatland insisting the midweek team had it all to play for. 'We are obviously hugely disappointed with the result [in the first Test] but it is important to regroup,' Gatland said. 'We know there are a lot of players motivated to go out and get a result for the whole group.

'A few players put their hands up for selection from the Chiefs game and played their way into the Test team so they know that there is another opportunity for them on Tuesday against the Super Rugby champions.'

The game ended in a dramatic 31-all draw, a yellow card for Iain Henderson proving costly as the Hurricanes came from behind. 'We had [Iain] Henderson off the field for ten minutes and conceded 14 points. To me that's the game in a nutshell,' Gatland added. Gatland also refused to use the bulk of his bench, admitting he was influenced by the backlash to his decision to call up players on a geographical basis.

Ahead of the second Test, Sam Warburton and Maro Itoje were drafted in to bolster the pack, while again Gatland threw a selectorial curve ball, pairing Owen Farrell and Johnny Sexton together in the midfield. Meanwhile, the Lions were focused on a vastly improved physical effort compared to the first Test in

BELOW Maro Itoje in line-out action in the second Test.

Auckland. 'They won [the physical] side of the game, there's no point in saying anything different, so that was obviously a big area for us where we let ourselves down,' admitted flanker Sean O'Brien. 'We drew a line in the sand during the week and spoke about the way we'd do things this week. It's about actions now.'

Despite the verbal sparring at the start of the week, Hansen attempted to play down the war of words between himself and Gatland, and criticised the *New Zealand Herald* for mocking up a picture of the Lions coach as a clown on the front page. 'To ridicule someone is not right,' Hansen said. 'It's disappointing really.' Gatland added: 'I think I have been pretty mild, and have tried to be complimentary of the All Blacks. I don't know if there is any hostility from this side. Hopefully we can have a good game of rugby and maybe enjoy a beer together afterwards.'

The match itself was an epic, edged by the Lions, who had a man advantage for most of the game after Sonny Bill Williams' red card. 'We didn't help ourselves by losing a player,' lamented Hansen. 'Whilst I am proud of our players for playing like that with 14 men, the Lions deserve the win.

'The referee made the call. Whether he called it right or wrong you've got to go with what he says.'

Lions captain Sam Warburton – influential after being recalled to the starting XV – was already looking ahead to the series decider back at Eden Park: 'I'll be happy next week when we bring the Test series home,' said the Welshman. 'We've got to win.'

THIRD TEST

Eden Park had not been breached since 1994, 38 victorious Tests in succession for the All Blacks. And now a draw, a little dent, but a dent nonetheless. That is a measure of the Lions' achievement

To bungee-jump or not to bungee-jump? That was the question in Queenstown for the British & Irish Lions. They had already taken a huge leap into the unknown with their victory in the second Test, so why not go for broke? They did just that, sanctioning the adrenalin-filled fix for those that did fancy a spot of adventure-driven R & R as they looked to rest and refuel ahead of the series-settling third Test in Auckland.

The Lions came in for a certain amount of criticism for their pre-planned three-day sojourn in the middle of the South Island. All Black flanker Jerome Kaino figured that he would 'rather be training', but in a way that is exactly what the Lions were doing. Kaino and his fellow All Blacks were only early- to mid-season in their labours whereas the Lions were at the end of a mammoth 11-month shift of work. Rest,

in whatever form it took, was of more use to them at this stage than yet more time on the training field. The Lions had done exactly the same four years earlier, decamping to the Queensland resort of Noosa ahead of the final Test in Sydney. It paid off then, and the Lions were confident that it would do so again.

As Brian Clough used to do to great effect with his Nottingham Forest footballers, famously taking them out for a few drinks (and perhaps more) on the eve of their European Cup final triumph against Malmö, so Gatland's approach to getting elite athletes to perform was part art, part science. There is no such thing as an infallible formula, but Gatland took his troops away on their South Island jolly armed with an array of statistics that gave all of them hope that they were doing the right thing.

The Lions had tailored their conditioning programme to make sure that their fitness levels were at the same high standard as those of the All Blacks. New Zealand invariably come through strongly in the last 20 minutes. The Lions front-loaded their training sessions at the start of the tour, working the players harder than normal, so as to be ready for these challenges in the Test series, particularly in the need to match the All Blacks stride for stride in the closing stages.

'The numbers [intensity and contact] are higher than we've ever seen but we've allowed for this,' said the head of strength and conditioning, Paul Stridgeon. 'This is the level we need to be to beat the All Blacks. We feel we took the All Blacks to a level in the second Test and we feel we'll be able to go higher again this weekend. We can be as intense as we want to be. We've got the momentum now.'

That certainly seemed to be the case in Wellington, although the fact that the All Blacks played with 14 men for a large part of the game did, self-evidently, have a bearing. But the Lions were in good spirits, training hard in the snow-capped surrounds of Queenstown before flying north. That they named an unchanged 23 reflected their upbeat mood. It was the first time since 1993 that the Lions had sent the same XV down the

LEFT All Blacks full back Jordie Barrett palms down a cross-kick from brother Beauden into the path of the oncoming Ngani Laumape (out of picture) for New Zealand's first try of the third Test.

PAGE 21 Referee Romain Poite explains to captains Read and Warburton why he is changing his 79th-minute decision against Ken Owens from a penalty to a scrum.

tunnel for a Test; indeed only the sixth time in their history that there had been no changes between Tests. In a neat reversal of fortunes New Zealand were once again forced to reshuffle as injury and suspension affected their plans. There were starting debuts for two Hurricanes players, full back Jordie Barrett and centre Ngani Laumape, while there was also a recall for the formidable Julian 'The Bus' Savea, scorer of 46 tries in 53 Tests and primed to take his considerable bulk down the Sexton–Farrell channel.

The stage was set. Gatland had implored his men to 'go out and do something special, create their own bit of history'. Auckland knew all about seizing the moment, having turned out in their thousands just days earlier to acclaim their returning America's Cup heroes. The Lions were intent, though, on raining on any rugby parade.

The series was locked at 1-1 and it was to remain that way after an elemental battle of skills and wills, Owen Farrell once again holding his nerve to strike the equalising penalty goal just three minutes before the end of an absorbing contest. The 15-15 scoreline did leave a deflated air around the ground after such a tumultuous series, but it was only right and proper on the night. The two sets of warriors had slugged each other to a standstill. Eden Park had not been breached since 1994, 38 victorious Tests in succession for the All Blacks. And now a draw, a little dent, but a dent nonetheless. That is a measure of the Lions' achievement.

The finale was not without its controversy. All Black captain Kieran Read ripped off his headband and hurled it to the floor, his frustration evident in that his team had been denied by a contentious call by referee Romain Poite two minutes from time. Poite had called a penalty against Lions hooker Ken Owens for handling a knock-on from a restart after Liam Williams had fumbled the take in the air. On reflection and TMO review, Poite determined that it was an accidental offside and so a scrum.

BELOW With just minutes to go, Owen Farrell converts yet another high-pressure kick – this time to square the series.

FACING PAGE Skippers Kieran Read and Sam Warburton take charge of the trophy together after the drawn series.

Once the officials began to study the replays on the big screen, other considerations began to take shape. Was Read ahead of the kicker at the restart? Had the All Black captain interfered with Williams as he tried to claim the ball? Did it in fact go forward? Under the protocol of the TMO, Poite ought not to have been weighing up such things as knock-ons. However, it was generally felt that the right outcome had been arrived at even if it had been by the wrong way. Well, that was the view in the northern hemisphere.

Read might also have vented his annoyance at his own side who created so much, particularly in the first half, but could not take full measure from such dominance, even if there were two tries from the starting debutants, centre Ngani Laumape and full back Jordie Barrett. In part that was credit to the Lions rush defence which caused the All Blacks difficulties right across the series, baffling them at times. But New Zealand were also culpable of making errors, a reflection of the inexperience in their back line.

Owen Farrell had a torrid evening in many regards, curiously out of kilter in his general play but reliable as ever with the boot, chipping away, chipping away. The Lions' return of five penalty goals was also helped by a monster 55-metre strike from Elliot Daly just seconds into the second half, a timely boost to morale.

It was the fabulous Barrett Boys who were the star-turn act on the night, the combo that had honed their skills on the Taranaki farmstead as kids. It was a Barrett double act that made the breakthrough, the brothers combining with ease in the 14th minute, Beauden hoisting it right, Jordie, the 6ft 5in giant, leaping above Daly to palm it down to Laumape, who scored.

The Lions were under the cosh for long stretches of the first half. New Zealand had countless half-chances but could not convert. The Lions did not let their heads drop, testimony to their togetherness. Farrell had another pot at goal in the 32nd minute and succeeded to narrow the gap to one point.

The scoreline did not last. Once again there was supreme skill involved, this time from Laumape who offloaded in the tackle to feed on to Anton Lienert-Brown who found Jordie Barrett in full flight to the line. The conversion was missed but the All Blacks looked comfortable with their 12-6 lead at the interval.

The Lions were living off scraps. On such meagre rations everything had to count. It did when Daly banged over that 55-metre effort within 80 seconds of the restart, but then they fluffed a line out with a not-straight throw following the yellow card shown to Jerome Kaino for a swinging arm in the tackle on Alun Wyn Jones. The Lions did not manage to capitalise until right at the end of the sin-binning, Farrell stroking over a penalty from 45 metres on the hour mark to level the scores at 12-12.

Then came the denouement. It was magnificent theatre. And for that we can all be grateful.

THIRD TEST: POINTS OF VIEW

So out of nowhere, we had a decider, as the delirious hordes of Lions fans prepared to flock north from Wellington to Auckland, via a stop or two on the way. There was the usual post-match incident as Sonny Bill Williams copped a ban for his shot on Anthony Watson, while Lions flanker Sean O'Brien was cited – and then cleared – for a challenge on Waisake Naholo. Hooker Jamie George helped set up the Lions' decisive try at the Westpac. 'We are fully aware of what is at stake,' George said the next day. 'It is going to be a fantastic occasion on Saturday and one again that we will never forget.

'I have said it before and I will say it again – we cannot get carried away with the emotional side of the game.'

The sentiment was echoed by New Zealand coach Steve Hansen in the week, who insisted Saturday's decider would not define his team. 'It's not the first time we've lost, every week there is pressure. We are expected to win every Test match, and when we win we are expected to win well. But we are only playing a rugby game,' Hansen said.

'Real pressure is giving someone CPR and trying to save their life and when that doesn't work telling their children or father or mother. That's real pressure. We could win, lose or draw, but we will be a better team for it. Is there any more pressure this week than last week? No, because we need to win to win the series.'

After naming an unchanged squad, Warren Gatland urged his men to seize the day at Eden Park. 'It's a chance to do something special. You have those moments in your life and you don't want those moments to pass you by,' he said. The match itself was another thriller. After threatening to run away with the Test match in the first half, the All Blacks were pegged back by the resilient Lions, who drew level at 15-all with minutes remaining, thanks to the irrepressible Owen Farrell. Then, controversy, as Romain Poite strangely watered down a decision to give New Zealand a penalty in the dying stages, after consultation with his team of officials. A drawn match, a drawn series, with no one quite knowing what to make of it all.

'We all know what happened and we all know what probably should have happened. It's a decision the ref has made and we will live with it,' said a philosophical Hansen. Gatland himself walked into a press conference wearing a clown's nose – a rare glimpse of humour on a challenging tour.

Ultimately for Gatland and the Lions, a drawn series was an outstanding result in the circumstances. 'Given the schedule, given how tough the tour was, to come to New Zealand and get a draw you've got to be proud of that,' Gatland added.

BELOW Elliot Daly launches his 55-metre howitzer shot just after the half-time break in the third Test at Eden Park.

VERDICT

The tourists were welcomed with open arms by the Kiwis who were relishing the prospect of seeing the All Blacks being given a serious challenge, which is exactly what they got

They said that it could not be done. They said the schedule was impossible. They said this and they said that, forever questioning the value of the Lions concept and undermining its very existence by placing ludicrous restrictions on the number of games to be played as well as the preparation time available.

There are those who would do away with the Lions, seeing them as something of an outdated throwback to the amateur era with their silly notions of proper tours with midweek games played against provincial teams. Sure, the players may love it, the bonding and the striving to reach peaks of excellence against the world's best, but what do they know? They are mere employees, given to the Lions by their paymasters, some more willingly than others.

The 2017 tour to New Zealand should be a watershed moment for the Lions. The English club officials who seek to reduce future tours to eight matches should be sent packing. Two (respectable) figures, Tony Rowe of Exeter Chiefs and Leicester's Simon Cohen, both voiced their serious reservations about the viability of the Lions project during this tour, stating that more money needed to be paid in compensation to the clubs and that the calendar was too cramped as it is and that tours should be shortened.

If one thing was proved on this trip it was that ten matches is a bare minimum to get a side in shape to face any of the southern hemisphere superpowers. Even then, Warren Gatland had to resort to summoning six players – the Geography Six as they became known in the media – from the nearest available tours, Wales in New Zealand and Scotland in Australia, so that they could do bench duties in the last two midweek matches. It was a desperate call by Warren Gatland, one that caused friction within the ranks, one that indicated just what strain Lions tours were under and will be under. If Gatland did not feel he had enough personnel at his disposal with 41 players taken to New Zealand, only four fewer than Clive Woodward took in 2005 to much criticism, then just how many might be needed to fulfil future tours?

Gatland should have simply called up players on merit, the likes of Joe Launchbury and Dylan Hartley, for example, on tour with England in Argentina, and have done with it. Don't blame Gatland for what he did. He was simply trying to work his way through a devilishly tricky situation.

The portents, though, are grim if that is what he has to resort to. The fear also is that the knockers will use the scenario as evidence that a ten-match tour is unsustainable. Hence the move to an eight-game itinerary, a project that has been accepted in principle by all the stakeholders involved in shaping the new global calendar which will come into play after the 2019 Rugby World Cup in Japan. It has been agreed in principle but is yet to be announced formally.

If it does come into play, it will be the death knell of Lions tours. An eight-game tour will be a Lions-lite experience, a semblance of a Lions tour but simply not the real thing. It took Gatland all the build-up games to settle on his best Test squad. Two players, Liam Williams and Elliot Daly, only truly declared themselves against the Chiefs in Hamilton in the last midweek game before the first Test; likewise, Courtney Lawes and Jack Nowell the following week against the Hurricanes in Wellington.

It is all very well taking note of how players are performing in training but it is only when the heat comes on during a game that you

BELOW Representatives of the Geography Six on the Lions bench against the Hurricanes. From left to right: Allan Dell, Kristian Dacey, Gareth Davies and Cory Hill. Finn Russell sits second from right between George Kruis and Leigh Halfpenny.

FACING PAGE Johnny Sexton, who took a while to find his form on tour, brings Ngani Laumape to a halt during the second Test.

PAGE 27 The power of red. A phalanx of Lions fans look on as Aaron Smith prepares to put the ball into a scrum during the third Test.

see their true colours. That process takes time, all the more so on this trip when those players involved in the first game against the Provincial Barbarians in Whangarei had to keep themselves awake on the bus to the ground as they battled jet lag only three days after arriving in the country. Also, several players, such as Johnny Sexton, took time to find their form. But find it they did.

The alternative is to pick a Test squad before the touring party leaves home shores. Those pre-selected Lions would put up a reasonable show but the strategy would not carry with it the same overtones for either player or supporter. It would be too much like the normal year in, year out set-up with international sides travelling the globe, flying in, preparing for a week and then playing a Test match. Nothing wrong with that. But that is not a Lions experience.

Pretty soon, the passionate investment from players would wane as would the commitment from those following these tours in their many thousands. It beggars belief that anyone would want to put in jeopardy such a success story as the Lions. Even those who would look to make a few quid out of it, and the clubs have every legitimate right to demand a fair share of the commercial cake for the release of their players, ought to realise that the profile of the 2017 Lions reached remarkable heights and that to threaten it is to commit hara-kiri. All media outlets reported a spike in interest over the six weeks, a sure-fire indicator that the Lions is good for business. There are many multinational companies round the world who would pay many hundreds of thousands of pounds to garner such coverage for their product. The English club game may operate in another part of the calendar with different imperatives and obligations but if it can't find a way to feed off the goodwill and interest generated, then it is not very good at its business.

The power brokers have to see the Lions as part of a holistic experience. It has a reach far beyond the sport's normal constituency, and rugby would be mad to spurn such a reality.

Part of the problem is that no one is vigorously fighting the Lions' corner in the committee rooms. There was not one dedicated representative at the World Rugby global gathering in San Francisco in January, a convention that made so many key decisions. Of course there were many there who spoke up on the Lions' behalf, but there was no one invited who was charged with defending their corner and their corner alone.

It is time to reappraise the move to an eight-game Lions tour. New Zealand 2017 has shown the way on many fronts. The tourists were welcomed with open arms by the Kiwis who were relishing the prospect of seeing the All Blacks being given a serious challenge, which is exactly what they got. Sir Graham Henry was not alone in the country rejoicing in the fact that there was a great sporting collision about to happen for which we could all be grateful.

For all the advances made down the years at spreading the word, a mission that has been enhanced by rugby's admission to the Olympic movement, it is still a niche sport. It has a presence in the marketplace but its appeal has pretty fixed parameters. The Lions stretch those boundaries, as was seen during this tour. It helped enormously that it was New Zealand, and not South Africa or Australia, in opposition, for the All Blacks, backed by Adidas, pride themselves on being a global brand. They attract interest even from those who know little of rugby.

But the 2017 British & Irish Lions matched them, stride for stride, point for point, until the teams could not be separated. It made for a compelling spectacle. And it would be absolute madness to place that in jeopardy.

BELOW With the greatest respect. The All Blacks and Lions after playing each other to a standstill in the final Test at Eden Park.

SCOREBOARD

3/6/2017 Whangarei

Prov B'barians 7
Try: Anderson-Heather (22)
Con: Gatland (23)

B&I Lions 13
Try: Watson (51)
Con: Farrell (53)
Pens: Sexton (16), Laidlaw (42)

15 Luteru Laulala	15 Stuart Hogg
14 Sam Vaka	14 Anthony Watson
13 Kaveinga Finau	13 Jonathan Joseph
12 Dwayne Sweeney	12 Ben Te'o
11 Sevu Reece	11 Tommy Seymour
10 Bryn Gatland	10 Jonathan Sexton
9 Jack Stratton	9 Greig Laidlaw
1 Aidan Ross	1 Joe Marler
2 S Anderson-Heather (c)	2 Rory Best
3 Oli Jager	3 Kyle Sinckler
4 Joshua Goodhue	4 Alun Wyn Jones
5 Keepa Mewett	5 Iain Henderson
6 James Tucker	6 Ross Moriarty
7 Lachlan Boshier	7 Sam Warburton (c)
8 Mitchell Dunshea	8 Taulupe Faletau
16 Andrew Makalio (41)	16 Jamie George (49)
17 Tolu Fahamokioa (49)	17 Mako Vunipola (49)
18 Marcel Renata (60)	18 Tadhg Furlong (49)
19 Matt Matich (45)	19 George Kruis (49)
20 Peter Rowe (60)	20 Justin Tipuric (66)
21 Richard Judd (53)	21 Rhys Webb (57)
22 Jonah Lowe (18)	22 Owen Farrell (48)
23 Joe Webber (57)	23 Elliot Daly

Referee Angus Gardner

7/6/2017 Auckland

Blues 22
Tries: R Ioane (6), Williams (40+2), West (73)
Cons: Perofeta (40+5), West (74)
Pen: West (52)

B&I Lions 16
Try: Stander (17)
Con: Halfpenny (18)
Pens: Halfpenny (24, 65, 70)

YC: Williams (56)

15 Michael Collins	15 Leigh Halfpenny
14 Matt Duffie	14 Jack Nowell
13 George Moala	13 Jared Payne
12 Sonny Bill Williams	12 Robbie Henshaw
11 Rieko Ioane	11 Elliot Daly
10 Stephen Perofeta	10 Dan Biggar
9 Augustine Pulu	9 Rhys Webb
1 Ofa Tu'ungafasi	1 Jack McGrath
2 James Parsons (c)	2 Ken Owens (c)
3 Charlie Faumuina	3 Dan Cole
4 Gerard Cowley-Tuioti	4 Maro Itoje
5 Scott Scrafton	5 Courtney Lawes
6 Akira Ioane	6 James Haskell
7 Blake Gibson	7 Justin Tipuric
8 Steven Luatua	8 CJ Stander
16 Epalahame Faiva (71)	16 Rory Best (68)
17 Alex Hodgman (57)	17 Joe Marler (53)
18 Sione Mafileo (57)	18 Kyle Sinckler (54)
19 Jimmy Tupou (57)	19 Iain Henderson (75)
20 Kara Pryor (65)	20 Peter O'Mahony (53)
21 Sam Nock (71)	21 Greig Laidlaw (75)
22 Ihaia West (51)	22 Jonathan Sexton (35)
23 Tinoai Faiane (40; 65)	23 Liam Williams (47)

Referee Pascal Gauzère

10/6/2017 Christchurch

Crusaders 3
Pen: Mo'unga (24)

B&I Lions 12
Pens: Farrell (12, 16, 30, 70)

15 Israel Dagg	15 Stuart Hogg
14 Seta Tamanivalu	14 George North
13 Jack Goodhue	13 Jonathan Davies
12 David Kaetau Havili	12 Ben Te'o
11 George Bridge	11 Liam Williams
10 Richie Mo'unga	10 Owen Farrell
9 Bryn Hall	9 Conor Murray
1 Joe Moody	1 Mako Vunipola
2 Codie Taylor	2 Jamie George
3 Owen Franks	3 Tadhg Furlong
4 Luke Romano	4 Alun Wyn Jones (c)
5 Sam Whitelock (c)	5 George Kruis
6 Heiden Bedwell-Curtis	6 Peter O'Mahony
7 Matt Todd	7 Sean O'Brien
8 Jordan Taufua	8 Taulupe Faletau
16 Ben Funnell (50)	16 Ken Owens (65)
17 Wyatt Crockett (50)	17 Jack McGrath (61)
18 Michael Alaalatoa (50)	18 Dan Cole (65)
19 Quinten Strange (55)	19 Maro Itoje (61)
20 Jed Brown (61)	20 CJ Stander (55)
21 M Drummond (61)	21 Rhys Webb
22 Mitch Hunt (73)	22 Jonathan Sexton (28)
23 Tim Bateman (65)	23 Anthony Watson (19)

Referee Mathieu Raynal

13/6/2017 Dunedin

Highlanders 23
Tries: Naholo (25), Coltman (59)
Cons: Sopoaga (26), Banks (61)
Pens: Sopoaga (4, 49), Banks (73)

B&I Lions 22
Tries: Joseph (29), Seymour (42), Warburton (52)
Cons: Biggar (30, 53)
Pen: Biggar (15)

15 Richard Buckman	15 Jared Payne
14 Waisake Naholo	14 Jack Nowell
13 Malakai Fekitoa	13 Jonathan Joseph
12 Teihorangi Walden	12 Robbie Henshaw
11 Tevita Li	11 Tommy Seymour
10 Lima Sopoaga	10 Dan Biggar
9 Kayne Hammington	9 Rhys Webb
1 Dan Lienert-Brown	1 Joe Marler
2 Liam Coltman	2 Rory Best
3 Siate Tokolahi	3 Kyle Sinckler
4 Alex Ainley	4 Courtney Lawes
5 Jackson Hemopo	5 Iain Henderson
6 Gareth Evans	6 James Haskell
7 Dillon Hunt	7 Sam Warburton (c)
8 Luke Whitelock (c)	8 CJ Stander
16 G Pleasants-Tate (67)	16 Ken Owens (24; 48)
17 Aki Seiuli (58)	17 Jack McGrath (54)
18 Siua Halanukonuka (67)	18 Dan Cole (48)
19 Josh Dickson (54)	19 Alun Wyn Jones (26)
20 James Lentjes (58)	20 Justin Tipuric (67)
21 Josh Renton (74)	21 Greig Laidlaw (47)
22 Marty Banks (11; 54)	22 Owen Farrell (67)
23 Patrick Osborne (67)	23 Elliot Daly (62)

Referee Angus Gardner

17/6/2017 Rotorua

Maori ABs 10
Try: Messam (11)
Con: McKenzie (12)
Pen: McKenzie (21)

YC: Kerr-Barlow (47)

B&I Lions 32
Tries: Pen try (50), Itoje (53)
Con: Halfpenny (55)
Pens: Halfpenny (4, 9, 19, 32, 43, 69)

15 James Lowe	15 Leigh Halfpenny
14 Nehe Milner-Skudder	14 Anthony Watson
13 Matt Proctor	13 Jonathan Davies
12 Charlie Ngatai	12 Ben Te'o
11 Rieko Ioane	11 George North
10 Damian McKenzie	10 Jonathan Sexton
9 Tawera Kerr-Barlow	9 Conor Murray
1 Kane Hames	1 Mako Vunipola
2 Ash Dixon (c)	2 Jamie George
3 Ben May	3 Tadhg Furlong
4 Joseph Wheeler	4 Maro Itoje
5 Thomas Franklin	5 George Kruis
6 Akira Ioane	6 Peter O'Mahony (c)
7 Elliot Dixon	7 Sean O'Brien
8 Liam Messam	8 Taulupe Faletau
16 Hikawera Elliot (69)	16 Ken Owens (64)
17 Chris Eves (61)	17 Jack McGrath (59)
18 Marcel Renata (69)	18 Kyle Sinckler (64)
19 Leighton Price (69)	19 Iain Henderson (59)
20 Kara Pryor (71)	20 Sam Warburton (63)
21 Bryn Hall (73)	21 Greig Laidlaw (66)
22 Ihaia West (66)	22 Dan Biggar (66)
23 Rob Thompson (53)	23 Elliot Daly (63)

Referee Jaco Peyper

20/6/2017 Hamilton

Chiefs 6
Pens: Donald (21, 40+1)

YC: Brown (54)

B&I Lions 34
Tries: Nowell (24, 58), Pen try (53), Payne (63)
Cons: Biggar (25, 59, 64)
Pens: Biggar (9, 17)

YC: Marler (12)

15 Shaun Stevenson	15 Liam Williams
14 Toni Pulu	14 Jack Nowell
13 Tim Nanai-Williams	13 Jared Payne
12 Jonathan Faauli	12 Robbie Henshaw
11 Solomona Alaimalo	11 Elliot Daly
10 Stephen Donald (c)	10 Dan Biggar
9 Finlay Christie	9 Greig Laidlaw
1 Siegfried Fisi'ihoi	1 Joe Marler
2 Liam Polwart	2 Rory Best (c)
3 Nepo Laulala	3 Dan Cole
4 Dominic Bird	4 Iain Henderson
5 Michael Allardice	5 Courtney Lawes
6 Mitchell Brown	6 James Haskell
7 Lachlan Boshier	7 Justin Tipuric
8 Tom Sanders	8 CJ Stander
16 Hikawera Elliot (59)	16 Kristian Dacey
17 Aidan Ross (64)	17 Allan Dell (13)
18 Atunaisa Moli (64)	18 Tomas Francis
19 Liam Messam (54)	19 Cory Hill
20 Mitch Karpik (64)	20 Alun Wyn Jones (51)
21 J Taumateine (57)	21 Gareth Davies
22 Luteru Laulala (65)	22 Finn Russell
23 Chase Tiatia (12)	23 Tommy Seymour (59)

Referee Jérôme Garcès

24/6/2017 Auckland

New Zealand 30
Tries: Taylor (17), Ioane (54, 69)
Cons: B Barrett (19, 55, 71)
Pens: B Barrett (13, 33, 60)

B&I Lions 15
Tries: O'Brien (35), Webb (80+1)
Con: Farrell (80+2)
Pen: Farrell (30)

15 Ben Smith	15 Liam Williams
14 Israel Dagg	14 Anthony Watson
13 Ryan Crotty	13 Jonathan Davies
12 Sonny Bill Williams	12 Ben Te'o
11 Rieko Ioane	11 Elliot Daly
10 Beauden Barrett	10 Owen Farrell
9 Aaron Smith	9 Conor Murray
1 Joe Moody	1 Mako Vunipola
2 Codie Taylor	2 Jamie George
3 Owen Franks	3 Tadhg Furlong
4 Brodie Retallick	4 Alun Wyn Jones
5 Sam Whitelock	5 George Kruis
6 Jerome Kaino	6 Peter O'Mahony (c)
7 Sam Cane	7 Sean O'Brien
8 Kieran Read (c)	8 Taulupe Faletau
16 Nathan Harris (66)	16 Ken Owens (67)
17 Wyatt Crockett (53)	17 Jack McGrath (51)
18 Charlie Faumuina (53)	18 Kyle Sinckler (58)
19 Scott Barrett (76)	19 Maro Itoje (47)
20 Ardie Savea (46)	20 Sam Warburton (53)
21 TJ Perenara (55)	21 Rhys Webb (67)
22 Aaron Cruden (26)	22 Jonathan Sexton (56)
23 A Lienert-Brown (33)	23 Leigh Halfpenny (71)

Referee Jaco Peyper

27/6/2017 Wellington

Hurricanes 31
Tries: Gibbins (26), Laumape (41), Goosen (67), Fifita (70)
Cons: Barrett (28, 42, 67, 70)
Pen: Barrett (49)
YC: Tahuriorangi (50)

B&I Lions 31
Tries: Seymour (17, 54), North (35)
Cons: Biggar (18, 37)
Pens: Biggar (9, 21, 30, 51)
YC: Henderson (65)

15 Jordie Barrett	15 Jack Nowell
14 Nehe Milner-Skudder	14 Tommy Seymour
13 Vince Aso	13 Jonathan Joseph
12 Ngani Laumape	12 Robbie Henshaw
11 Julian Savea	11 George North
10 Otere Black	10 Dan Biggar
9 Te Toiroa Tahuriorangi	9 Greig Laidlaw
1 Ben May	1 Joe Marler
2 Ricky Riccitelli	2 Rory Best (c)
3 Jeff Toomaga-Allen	3 Dan Cole
4 Mark Abbott	4 Iain Henderson
5 Sam Lousi	5 Courtney Lawes
6 Vaea Fifita	6 James Haskell
7 Callum Gibbins	7 Justin Tipuric
8 Brad Shields (c)	8 CJ Stander
16 Leni Apisai (61)	16 Kristian Dacey
17 Chris Eves (55)	17 Allan Dell
18 Michael Kainga	18 Tomas Francis
19 James Blackwell	19 Cory Hill
20 Reed Prinsep (55)	20 George Kruis (53)
21 K Hauiti-Parapara (68)	21 Gareth Davies
22 Wes Goosen (61)	22 Finn Russell (42)
23 Cory Jane (68)	23 Leigh Halfpenny (18)

Referee Romain Poite

1/7/2017 Wellington

New Zealand 21
Pens: B Barrett (19, 31, 36, 47, 53, 57, 66)

RC: Williams (24)

B&I Lions 24
Tries: Faletau (59), Murray (68)
Con: Farrell (69)
Pens: Farrell (22, 33, 40+2, 77)

YC: Vunipola (55)

15 Israel Dagg	15 Liam Williams
14 Waisake Naholo	14 Anthony Watson
13 Anton Lienert-Brown	13 Jonathan Davies
12 Sonny Bill Williams	12 Owen Farrell
11 Rieko Ioane	11 Elliot Daly
10 Beauden Barrett	10 Jonathan Sexton
9 Aaron Smith	9 Conor Murray
1 Joe Moody	1 Mako Vunipola
2 Codie Taylor	2 Jamie George
3 Owen Franks	3 Tadhg Furlong
4 Brodie Retallick	4 Maro Itoje
5 Sam Whitelock	5 Alun Wyn Jones
6 Jerome Kaino	6 Sam Warburton (c)
7 Sam Cane	7 Sean O'Brien
8 Kieran Read (c)	8 Taulupe Faletau
16 Nathan Harris (79)	16 Ken Owens
17 Wyatt Crockett (52)	17 Jack McGrath (63)
18 Charlie Faumuina (52)	18 Kyle Sinckler (61)
19 Scott Barrett (72)	19 Courtney Lawes (58)
20 Ardie Savea (63)	20 CJ Stander
21 TJ Perenara (65)	21 Rhys Webb
22 Aaron Cruden (59)	22 Ben Te'o
23 Ngani Laumape (26)	23 Jack Nowell (24)

Referee Jérôme Garcès

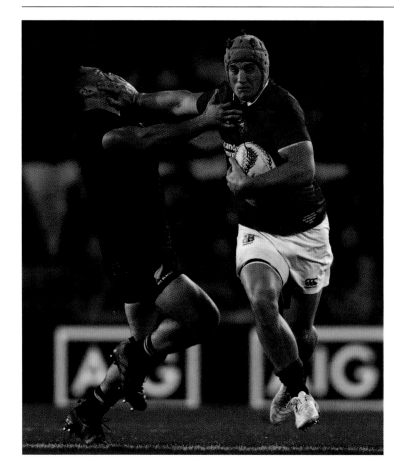

8/7/2017 Auckland

New Zealand 15
Tries: Laumape (14), J Barrett (35)
Con: B Barrett (15)
Pen: B Barrett (67)

YC: Kaino (49)

B&I Lions 15
Pens: Farrell (20, 32, 59, 77), Daly (41)

15 Jordie Barrett	15 Liam Williams
14 Israel Dagg	14 Anthony Watson
13 Anton Lienert-Brown	13 Jonathan Davies
12 Ngani Laumape	12 Owen Farrell
11 Julian Savea	11 Elliot Daly
10 Beauden Barrett	10 Jonathan Sexton
9 Aaron Smith	9 Conor Murray
1 Joe Moody	1 Mako Vunipola
2 Codie Taylor	2 Jamie George
3 Owen Franks	3 Tadhg Furlong
4 Brodie Retallick	4 Maro Itoje
5 Sam Whitelock	5 Alun Wyn Jones
6 Jerome Kaino	6 Sam Warburton (c)
7 Sam Cane	7 Sean O'Brien
8 Kieran Read (c)	8 Taulupe Faletau
16 Nathan Harris (72)	16 Ken Owens (69)
17 Wyatt Crockett (57)	17 Jack McGrath (59)
18 Charlie Faumuina (57)	18 Kyle Sinckler (59)
19 Scott Barrett (77)	19 Courtney Lawes (49)
20 Ardie Savea (59)	20 CJ Stander (41)
21 TJ Perenara (73)	21 Rhys Webb (69)
22 Aaron Cruden (72)	22 Ben Te'o (48; 72)
23 Malakai Fekitoa (66)	23 Jack Nowell (72)

Referee Romain Poite

LEFT Jonathan Davies, voted Lions players' player of the tour, in action in the first Test.